Eight Nights

On the first night of Chanukah, our family uses
the shamash candle from the middle
of the menorah to light one candle.

Our uncle tells us the Chanukah story.

On the second night of Chanukah,
our family lights two candles on the menorah.

Our aunt makes potato pancakes.
We call them latkes.

**On the third night of Chanukah,
our family lights three candles on the menorah.**

We play a game with a top.
We call the top a dreidel.

On the fourth night of Chanukah,
our family lights four candles on the menorah.

We sing songs together.

On the fifth night of Chanukah,
our family lights five candles on the menorah.

We have a big feast.

**On the sixth night of Chanukah,
our family lights six candles on the menorah.**

We get bags full of chocolate coins.
We call the coins Chanukah gelt.

On the seventh night of Chanukah,
our family lights seven candles on the menorah.

We go to our grandmother's house for dinner.
We call her Bubbie.

The eighth night of Chanukah is the last night.
Our family lights all the candles on the menorah!